The Enneagram Journ

MW00884633

"All constructs are wrong, but some are helpful" –George Box

So you know your enneagram type, but now what? The enneagram is a path to self-growth, but how do you do the work that this growth requires? This books serves as a guide to lead you through the introspective work of the enneagram. There are 9 different sections to this journal, listed in order from type 1 to type 9. Each section has journal prompts to help you process and apply the knowledge of your type to your life.

The enneagram is only as helpful as you allow it to be. If you don't do the self-reflection it requires it will just serve as a tool to inflate your ego. However, if you do the work your life will change and you will be able to get out of the box that you have been putting yourself into all this time. This journal is meant to serve as a way to process why you do what you do and to open you up to the possibility that your way of thinking is not the only way.

My work as a therapist has taught me that great questions are invaluable. They teach us about ourselves and about the world around us. I had the idea to create this journal because I saw that so many of my clients wanted to process their childhood, their work-life and their relationships and friendships, but were at a loss as to how to do this. Journaling is a great therapeutic technique because it not only allows you to process, but you are also able to conform it to your own needs. Not every prompt in this journal will apply to you. That is okay, dive deep into the questions that do resonate and attempt them honestly.

This journal has at least 50 prompts for each type to process. The questions are in no particular order. There is space below each question to write down your responses, but if more room is required feel free to use a notebook to record your questions. This journal will be what you make it, I hope you use it to change and challenge you and lead you to a greater understanding of yourself.

Type 1//The Perfectionist

How do you judge yourself? Do you compare yourself with others?

_____
_____
_____
_____
_____

How does your inner critic make you feel?

_____
_____
_____
_____
_____

What mission do you feel you must complete?

_____
_____
_____
_____
_____

Do you often feel you must justify your actions to others and to yourself?

_____
_____
_____
_____
_____

When do you get caught up in overthinking?

_____
_____
_____
_____
_____

Whose validation do you crave the most in life?

_____
_____
_____
_____
_____

How do you control your instinctual drives? Where could you be more lenient?

_____
_____
_____
_____
_____

How do you repress yourself? What is one thing you could stop repressing?

_____
_____
_____
_____
_____

Where in life do you get the most caught up in perfectionism?

_____
_____
_____
_____
_____

How are you strict with yourself? How are you strict with others?

_____
_____
_____
_____
_____

Do you trust your inner voice and what it tells you?

_____

_____

_____

_____

_____

Did you grow up too fast? What led to you to doing so?

_____

_____

_____

_____

_____

Did you feel the need to justify your existence at a young age?

_____

_____

_____

_____

_____

In what ways are you burned-out? What actions led to your burnout? How can you prevent future burnouts?

_____

_____

_____

_____

_____

How did your relationship with your parents feed into your perfectionism?

_____

_____

_____

_____

Were you the "voice of reason" in your family? How did this affect you?

_____

_____

_____

_____

_____

What emotions come up for you when you make an error?

_____

_____

_____

_____

_____

What emotions come up for you when someone else catches your error before you do?

_____

_____

_____

_____

_____

Were you a serious child? How did this affect how you related to others?

_____

_____

_____

_____

_____

What kind of pressures did your parents put on you as a child?

_____

_____

_____

_____

_____

How have you felt disconnected from the "protective figures" in your life (often the biological father)?

_____

_____

_____

_____

_____

Did you have to take care of others in your family unit at a young age? How did this affect you?

_____
_____
_____
_____
_____

How did you have to "father yourself" or "mother yourself"?

_____
_____
_____
_____
_____

How do you try and surpass other's expectations of you? How does this manifest itself in your life?

_____
_____
_____
_____
_____

Do you often view others as immature? What kinds of people trigger you?

_____
_____
_____
_____
_____

Where in life do you have black and white thinking? Where do you have grey thinking?

_____
_____
_____
_____
_____

Does the statement "If I don't do this no one else will" resonate with you?

_____
_____
_____
_____
_____

Does the statement "No one will do this as well as I can so I must complete it" resonate with you?

_____
_____
_____
_____
_____

Do you feel like you are a burden when you ask for help? How can you move past this fear?

_____
_____
_____
_____
_____

How does having control of your environment make you feel? What would happen if you lost this control?

_____
_____
_____
_____
_____

What do you find beautiful about your flaws?

_____
_____
_____
_____

How do you try to "fix" others? Do you have someone who you always try to fix?

_____
_____
_____
_____
_____

Whose lackadaisical ways of doing things bother you most?

_____
_____
_____
_____
_____

Do you make time for self-care? What gets in the way?

_____
_____
_____
_____
_____

Where do you find yourself being most impatient?

_____
_____
_____
_____
_____

How do you react when those around you are cutting corners?

_____
_____
_____
_____
_____

What makes you most angry? Do you let yourself fully feel this emotion?

_____
_____
_____
_____
_____

How might you allow yourself to feel your anger and not suppress it or justify it?

_____

_____

_____

_____

_____

How does getting caught up on the details stop you from enjoying the good things in life?

_____

_____

_____

_____

_____

What do you view as the "good" parts of you and what do you view the "bad" parts?

_____

_____

_____

_____

_____

Where do you hold your tension in your body? How could you mediate this?

_____

_____

_____

_____

_____

Do you find yourself raising your standards when you get close to meeting the goals you set out for yourself?

_____

_____

_____

_____

_____

When do you have the hardest time relaxing? Do you feel the need to "earn" your relaxation time?

_____

_____

_____

_____

_____

How many times a day are you disappointed with yourself and others?

_____
_____
_____
_____
_____

What is really at stake when you start feeling frantic about a goal you have set? Is your level of frustration with yourself appropriate for the situation at hand?

_____
_____
_____
_____
_____

What is your self-talk like? What do you say to yourself?

_____
_____
_____
_____
_____

Who are you trying to please? Yourself? Everyone else?

_____
_____
_____
_____
_____

What have vacations or times off been like for you? Can you truly relax or do you feel the need to constantly be doing?

_____
_____
_____
_____
_____

Do you feel like you are wasting time if you are not improving yourself? What are examples of this?

_____

_____

_____

_____

_____

Do you feel that you must be good to be loved and that good is equated with "rightness"?

_____

_____

_____

_____

_____

How has your ability to point out errors and better ways to do things served you?

_____

_____

_____

_____

_____

When have your attempts to point out errors been taken the wrong way by those around you?

_____

_____

_____

_____

_____

How important is "being right" to you? What feelings come up when you are proven wrong?

_____

_____

_____

_____

_____

How does "order" play out in your life? Compulsive cleaning? Is it complete control of your schedule or specific procedures in the workplace?

_____
_____
_____
_____
_____

What kind of disorder most annoys you?

_____
_____
_____
_____
_____

Do you have any guilt, shame or anxiety about your body or bodily functions? What would it look like to validate your human needs?

_____
_____
_____
_____
_____

What do you use to "escape" from daily life? Do you find this to be positive or negative?

_____
_____
_____
_____
_____

What do you see as your biggest shortcoming? What is your biggest strength? Do these relate to one another?

_____
_____
_____
_____
_____

What "defects" in yourself have you repressed as to not deal with them?

_____
_____
_____
_____
_____

How has the judgment of others limited your view of those around you?

_____
_____
_____
_____
_____

How has the judgment of yourself limited your sense of inner peace?

_____
_____
_____
_____
_____

Write down a list of your judgments towards yourself and others. Do you see a theme?

_____
_____
_____
_____
_____

Write about a time it was hard to accept criticism from someone in your life. How could you be gentler with yourself?

_____
_____
_____
_____
_____

How have you handled outcomes that were not as "perfect" as you had hoped? Did you let this take the happiness out of what could have still been a positive outcome?

_____

_____

_____

_____

_____

What do your daydreams consist of? Have you made any of these dreams a reality?

_____

_____

_____

_____

_____

What have been the turning points in your life?

_____

_____

_____

_____

_____

Who in your life are you able to hear criticism from?

_____

_____

_____

_____

_____

How has your strong sense of self-discipline helped you in life?

_____

_____

_____

_____

_____

What is a problem you see around you or in your community? How could you contribute to fixing it?

_____
_____
_____
_____
_____

What is your relationship with your own anger? Do you suppress it? Are you afraid of it?

_____
_____
_____
_____
_____

What part of you do you need to work on accepting?

_____
_____
_____
_____
_____

When you are stressed do you find yourself getting caught up in daydreams of how things could be?

_____
_____
_____
_____
_____

When you are stressed do you relate to the statement, "Everyone is having a better time than me"?

_____
_____
_____
_____
_____

In stress do you ever find yourself pouting, experiencing jealousy or resentments? What do you do to recover from these feelings?

_____
_____
_____
_____
_____

Type 2//The Helper

How has your attention and energy been going to the needs of others?

_____

_____

_____

_____

_____

How do you support or nurture yourself?

_____

_____

_____

_____

_____

How do you allow others to support you?

_____

_____

_____

_____

_____

In what ways do you feel or act as though you were indispensable? Do you take pride in being needed?

_____

_____

_____

_____

_____

In what ways do you alter or change yourself to fit what others seem to want?

_____

_____

_____

_____

_____

How do you express humility?

_____
_____
_____
_____
_____

Do you find yourself trying to win people over? What does this do for you?

_____
_____
_____
_____
_____

How have you embraced the dark side of yourself? Has this been tricky for you?

_____
_____
_____
_____
_____

Do you sacrifice yourself for others in hopes of their validation?

_____
_____
_____
_____
_____

How have you manipulated others to get your emotional needs met?

_____
_____
_____
_____
_____

What things or people do you look to for your self-worth?

_____
_____
_____
_____
_____

What resentments are you carrying with you from people who have not reciprocated your love and service?

_____
_____
_____
_____
_____

What needs of your own are you repressing?

_____
_____
_____
_____
_____

How do you feel when you are not rewarded for your sacrifices?

_____
_____
_____
_____
_____

How do you relate to the phrase, "You need to give in order to get"?

_____
_____
_____
_____
_____

How would your relationships change if you stopped trying to earn other's love?

_____
_____
_____
_____
_____

What kind of self care activities do you need to do to be at your best?

_____
_____
_____
_____
_____

What needs, hurts and self-doubts have you repressed? How could you start to acknowledge them?

_____

_____

_____

_____

_____

Did you get a message in childhood that said "to acknowledge your own needs is to be selfish"?

_____

_____

_____

_____

_____

Do you find yourself trying to "fix" others?

_____

_____

_____

_____

_____

Do you acknowledge your own pain or do you deflect and focus only on the pain of others?

_____

_____

_____

_____

_____

Are any of your current relationships codependent in nature? Have you had codependent relationships in the past?

_____

_____

_____

_____

_____

What is your relationship like with food? What is your relationship like with your body? Do you view yourself as worthy of being taken care of?

_____

_____

_____

_____

_____

What do you fear will happen if people don't like you?

_____

_____

_____

_____

_____

In what ways do you try and win the approval of others?

_____

_____

_____

_____

_____

Do you feel that you must be noticed to be validated?

_____

_____

_____

_____

_____

Does giving advice give you an ego boost?

_____

_____

_____

_____

_____

How do you enable others? How has this affected your relationships?

_____

_____

_____

_____

_____

Do you see a pattern in the type of people you like to win over?

_____
_____
_____
_____
_____

Do you struggle with feeling like you are "not enough"?

_____
_____
_____
_____
_____

Do you ever find yourself playing the victim or the martyr?

_____
_____
_____
_____
_____

In what ways do you find yourself people pleasing?

_____
_____
_____
_____
_____

Do you feel the need to be close to those around you? What does this protect you from?

_____
_____
_____
_____
_____

What emotional wounds are you hiding by your seemingly selfless acts?

_____
_____
_____
_____
_____

How do you receive love? How do you give love?

_____
_____
_____
_____
_____

Do you expect others to respond to you in a certain way? How could you allow others to respond more freely to you?

_____
_____
_____
_____
_____

Do you ever come on too strong in your relationships? How do others react?

_____
_____
_____
_____
_____

Do you have healthy boundaries in what you ask of others? What about what you allow others to ask of you?

_____
_____
_____
_____
_____

How do you overextend yourself?

_____
_____
_____
_____
_____

Can you think of a relationship where you feel possessive or the need to control the other person? What is this rooted in?

_____

_____

_____

_____

_____

How has your health suffered from overextending yourself? Did this serve as "proof" that you are a martyr and make you feel justified?

_____

_____

_____

_____

_____

How could you better listen to your body? What kind of symptoms do you usually have when you are pushing yourself too far?

_____

_____

_____

_____

_____

When you are stressed do you find yourself becoming more direct and forceful? Does this surprise the people around you?

_____

_____

_____

_____

_____

How can you become less concerned about what other people think of you?

_____

_____

_____

_____

_____

What do you need to say "no" to?

_____
_____
_____
_____
_____

How could you start to evaluate your motives behind helping others? Do you ever give too much and then regret it because it was not for the right reasons?

_____
_____
_____
_____
_____

What do you find yourself being most disappointed about?

_____
_____
_____
_____
_____

How could you learn to accept all of your emotions, even the bad ones without censoring them?

_____
_____
_____
_____
_____

Do you respond quickly to your own needs or do you put those on the backburner and only address the needs of others?

_____
_____
_____
_____
_____

Do you expect those who are close to you to know what you need without you having to tell them?

_____
_____
_____
_____
_____

Type 3//The Achiever

In what ways have you been adjusting yourself to meet the expectations of others?

_____
_____
_____
_____
_____

What do you want recognition for?

_____
_____
_____
_____
_____

How do you deceive yourself? How do you deceive others?

_____
_____
_____
_____
_____

How do you avoid failure?

_____
_____
_____
_____
_____

How do you focus on doing versus being?

_____
_____
_____
_____
_____

What happens when your feelings come up? What are you feeling now?

_____
_____
_____
_____
_____

What activities were valued by your peers and parents when you were a child? How important was it for you to excel in these activities?

_____
_____
_____
_____
_____

As a child and even now do you feel like you need to be someone else to be accepted?

_____
_____
_____
_____
_____

How has success given you worth?

_____
_____
_____
_____
_____

How much of your life is made up of you adapting to others expectations of you?

_____
_____
_____
_____
_____

What did you do extremely well growing up? How did the validation you received fuel you?

_____
_____
_____
_____
_____

How does the statement "It is not okay to be not okay" resonate with you?

_____
_____
_____
_____
_____

Do you have workaholic tendencies? How do you keep these in check?

_____
_____
_____
_____
_____

When have you experienced burnout? What was this like for you? How did you recover?

_____
_____
_____
_____
_____

How important is attractiveness to you? In yourself? In others?

_____
_____
_____
_____
_____

What makes you successful? How has this shaped who you are?

_____
_____
_____
_____
_____

How could you let go of the idea that your value is dependent on the positive regard of others?

_____
_____
_____
_____
_____

When have you felt the desire to outshine others? Have you often worried that other people's achievements will overshadow your own?

_____
_____
_____
_____
_____

How have you projected an image of yourself to others that simply is not true? How could you integrate your true self with your ego self?

_____
_____
_____
_____
_____

When have you pushed down your emotions in order to keep up with the image of success that you want others to see?

_____
_____
_____
_____
_____

When have you found yourself in competition with those around you? Do you fear being overshadowed by someone else?

_____
_____
_____
_____
_____

Do you want affirmation and recognition from the same people who you hope to outshine?

_____
_____
_____
_____
_____

Why do you have the goals that you have? What is at the root of your desire to achieve them?

_____

_____

_____

_____

_____

When have you found yourself involved in projects that you were not interested because of your need to compete or to prove yourself?

_____

_____

_____

_____

_____

How do you handle your failures? How do you reframe them?

_____

_____

_____

_____

_____

What image are you projecting to your friends, colleges and family? Are they all the same image or do they differ in some way?

_____

_____

_____

_____

_____

Do you find yourself fearing intimacy with those around you because you want to maintain an image of success? What is it like for you when others find out you don't have it all together?

_____

_____

_____

_____

_____

When you are stressed do you become complacent, burned-out and apathetic? How do you combat these feelings?

_____
_____
_____
_____
_____

What do you do to relax? Is it hard for you to relax or does it come easily to you?

_____
_____
_____
_____
_____

Do you catch yourself "turning it on" for the people around you or has this become second nature to you?

_____
_____
_____
_____
_____

Who can you be vulnerable with? Who can you share your anxieties with? Is this list shorter than you would like?

_____
_____
_____
_____
_____

Do you have any hobbies that are just for you and not used to impress anyone? If not, could this benefit you?

_____
_____
_____
_____
_____

How do you help those around you be their best?

_____
_____
_____
_____
_____

Are you willing to risk losing the approval of others to follow your own heart?

_____
_____
_____
_____
_____

How could you take better care of yourself?

_____
_____
_____
_____
_____

What were you told in childhood that made you feel the need to succeed?

_____
_____
_____
_____
_____

When have you cut corners in the past?

_____
_____
_____
_____
_____

What are vacations or times off like for you? Are you able to slow down?

_____
_____
_____
_____
_____

Do you pride yourself in being able to connect with anyone?

_____
_____
_____
_____
_____

Do you keep a close eye on how people are reacting to you?

_____
_____
_____
_____
_____

Do you often feel disconnected from your emotions?

_____
_____
_____
_____
_____

How could you work to connect with how you are feeling?

_____
_____
_____
_____
_____

How do you relate to the statement, "Life is about getting things done"?

_____
_____
_____
_____
_____

Who are your biggest role models in life? What characteristics to these people have in common?

_____
_____
_____
_____
_____

Do you find yourself being slothful when you get stressed?

_____
_____
_____
_____
_____

Is it harder for you to follow then to lead?

_____
_____
_____
_____
_____

How could you slow down?

_____
_____
_____
_____
_____

What makes you feel the most rested and rejuvenated?

_____
_____
_____
_____
_____

Who can you be vulnerable with?

_____
_____
_____
_____
_____

When do you feel most restless?

_____
_____
_____
_____

Type 4//The Romantic

How have you focused your attention and energy on what is missing?

_____
_____
_____
_____
_____

In what ways do you experience a sense of longing or envy?

_____
_____
_____
_____
_____

How have you diminished or disdained the ordinary or mundane?

_____
_____
_____
_____
_____

Do you feel pride in being special or unique, or feel shame in being less than your ideal?

_____
_____
_____
_____
_____

In what ways have you felt misunderstood?

_____
_____
_____
_____
_____

Have you stayed true to yourself?

_____
_____
_____
_____
_____

How have you formed your identity around your inner experience?

_____
_____
_____
_____
_____

What brings you significance in life right now?

_____
_____
_____
_____
_____

What would bring you significance in your "ideal" life?

_____
_____
_____
_____
_____

How are you fundamentally different from others?

_____
_____
_____
_____
_____

Are you in touch with your suffering? How has it made you who you are?

_____
_____
_____
_____
_____

Do you ever find yourself building your identity around how different you are from the people around you?

_____
_____
_____
_____
_____

What fantasies do you have about yourself? In what way do these fantasies protect you from how you truly feel?

_____
_____
_____
_____
_____

When do you feel most creative?

_____
_____
_____
_____
_____

Who knows you best? How is this relationship different from others?

_____
_____
_____
_____
_____

In what ways are you romantic?

_____
_____
_____
_____
_____

How do you romanticize your past experiences?

_____
_____
_____
_____
_____

Do you need to brood over your negative feelings before you can be rid of them? What could speed this process up?

_____
_____
_____
_____
_____

Do you ever feel alone in a room full of people? How could you increase connection to others?

_____
_____
_____
_____
_____

Do you find it hard to be apart of projects if you do not have creative control?

_____
_____
_____
_____
_____

Would others call you dramatic? How does that sit with you?

_____
_____
_____
_____
_____

Do you find yourself imagining scenes or conversations that have not happened yet?

_____
_____
_____
_____
_____

Do you prefer to work alone or with others? Why do you think this is?

_____

_____

_____

_____

_____

Are you motivated by finding yourself? How has this served you?

_____

_____

_____

_____

_____

Are you in touch with your intuition? How has this helped you?

_____

_____

_____

_____

_____

Do you feel that you are being true to your emotional needs? If not what would help get you there?

_____

_____

_____

_____

_____

Do you focus on your personal flaws and deficiencies more than what is healthy?

_____

_____

_____

_____

_____

Do you hold on to past hurts? What helps you to process and let go?

_____

_____

_____

_____

_____

Do you feel disconnected from your parents? How has this affected your identity formation?

_____
_____
_____
_____
_____

Who do you feel seen by? What qualities about them make you feel affirmed?

_____
_____
_____
_____
_____

Are you waiting for others to "redeem" you with their love?

_____
_____
_____
_____
_____

Do you find yourself being particular about your physical surroundings? What does your ideal space look like?

_____
_____
_____
_____
_____

Are you drawn to relationships that are emotionally intense? What does this do for you?

_____
_____
_____
_____
_____

Do you allow emotional whims to dictate your behavior? Has this gotten you into any trouble?

_____
_____
_____
_____
_____

How do you cope with the emotional highs and lows in your life? Is it healthy or unhealthy coping?

_____
_____
_____
_____
_____

When do you overindulge? Are there certain things you go to again and again for comfort?

_____
_____
_____
_____
_____

What makes you unique? Do you view these traits as a blessing or a curse?

_____
_____
_____
_____
_____

Do you envy the happiness of others? How does this affect you?

_____
_____
_____
_____
_____

Who do you compare yourself to? How does this comparison make you feel about yourself?

_____
_____
_____
_____
_____

Do you fantasize about a rescuer or someone who could save you from your current circumstances? What is this person like?

_____
_____
_____
_____
_____
_____

How do you relate to the statement "I am what I feel"?

_____
_____
_____
_____
_____
_____

How could you become more grounded to the "real world" and become less stuck in your imagination?

_____
_____
_____
_____
_____
_____

How could you start to let go of the belief that you are more flawed than those around you? What would this take?

_____
_____
_____
_____
_____
_____

Do you fear that you are wasting your life? What gives you meaning?

_____
_____
_____
_____
_____

How much of your self-imagine is based off of how unlike other people you are?

_____
_____
_____
_____
_____

In what ways do you stay true to yourself?

_____
_____
_____
_____
_____

In what ways do you break the rules? Do you ever feel as though rules do not apply to you?

_____
_____
_____
_____
_____

Have you ever felt like normal aspects of life such as work or family life have gotten in the way of your search for self?

_____
_____
_____
_____
_____

Do you feel flawed in comparison to those around you? What evidence do you have to back this thought up?

_____
_____
_____
_____
_____

Who do you most compare yourself to? Why do you think this is?

_____
_____
_____
_____
_____

How do you cultivate environments that reflect the feelings you identify with? What about these spaces make you feel at home?

_____
_____
_____
_____
_____

How do you cope with your feelings of envy? Does this manifest as aloofness or distance from others?

_____
_____
_____
_____
_____

What qualities do you fantasize about having? What steps could you take to actually acquire these qualities?

_____
_____
_____
_____
_____

Do you search for hidden meaning in the things people say? How does this lead to resentments?

_____
_____
_____
_____
_____

When do you feel most self-conscious? Do these feelings every stop you from doing things you want or need to do?

_____

_____

_____

_____

_____

Who do you look to for support with your emotional needs? Do you also support this person with their emotions?

_____

_____

_____

_____

_____

What is at the root of you withholding yourself from others? When do you feel like this is a legitimate choice when are you using this as a means of self-protection?

_____

_____

_____

_____

_____

Have you formed your identity around having problems? How have you over identified with suffering?

_____

_____

_____

_____

_____

Do you have an unconscious attachment to having difficulties? Who would you be without these difficulties?

_____

_____

_____

_____

_____

Did you have to use your emotions to get attention as a child such as having temper tantrums or throwing fits?

_____
_____
_____
_____
_____

How could you move away from looking at your "feelings as facts"?

_____
_____
_____
_____
_____

Do you have a hard time following through on your dreams? What is standing in your way?

_____
_____
_____
_____
_____

What talents do you daydream most about possessing? How could you take the time to cultivate one of these talents?

_____
_____
_____
_____
_____

Do you have anyone in your life who keeps you in line? Do you benefits from these reality checks?

_____
_____
_____
_____
_____

Do you ever catch yourself using friends as a dumping ground for your emotional problems? Do you take the time to listen to their problems as well?

_____

_____

_____

_____

_____

Are you connected to your intuition? How does this serve you?

_____

_____

_____

_____

_____

How would life change if you grounded yourself in your present moment? What are some ways you could do this?

_____

_____

_____

_____

_____

Type 5//The Investigator

In what ways do you react when you feel intruded upon?

_____
_____
_____
_____
_____

How do you maintain a sense of safety by erecting boundaries and limiting contact with others?

_____
_____
_____
_____
_____

How do you avoid emotions and stay in your head?

_____
_____
_____
_____
_____

When do you fall into analysis paralysis?

_____
_____
_____
_____
_____

How do you minimize your wants and desires?

_____
_____
_____
_____
_____

How are you withholding or stingy?

_____

_____

_____

_____

_____

When do you find yourself going inward the most?

_____

_____

_____

_____

_____

Who do you give your time to?

_____

_____

_____

_____

_____

What role does "learning" play in your life?

_____

_____

_____

_____

_____

What things do you consider yourself an expert at?

_____

_____

_____

_____

_____

What do kind of things do you feel incompetent at? How do you cope with these feelings?

_____

_____

_____

_____

_____

When do you most isolate yourself?

_____

_____

_____

_____

_____

Are you often drawn to things that are unconventional or unusual?

_____

_____

_____

_____

_____

Do you distract yourself from areas of life you feel you are not competent at?

_____

_____

_____

_____

_____

Does dealing with physical matters feel daunting to you? How do you cope with this?

_____

_____

_____

_____

_____

Has it been a challenge for you to pursue whatever questions and problems excite you as well as maintain relationships and take care of yourself?

_____

_____

_____

_____

_____

Did you have a fear of being overwhelmed by your parents as a child? Did you cope with this by going inward where it was "safe"?

_____
_____
_____
_____
_____

How important is independence to you?

_____
_____
_____
_____
_____

Did you learn to cut off from painful feelings of need and longing (usually feelings toward parent or caregiver) by staying in your mind at an early age?

_____
_____
_____
_____
_____

Do you feel drained by social interactions? What helps you to recharge?

_____
_____
_____
_____
_____

How could you start to let go of the belief that you are separate from your environment?

_____
_____
_____
_____
_____

In what areas of your life do you feel unsure of yourself?

_____
_____
_____
_____
_____

Do you feel protective of the niche you are highly knowledgeable about? When have others impeded upon your territory?

_____
_____
_____
_____
_____

Do you find yourself analyzing the world around you instead of directly experiencing it?

_____
_____
_____
_____
_____

Do your ideas give you a temporary sense of confidence?

_____
_____
_____
_____
_____

When you feel insecure do you find yourself wanting others to see you as an expert at something?

_____
_____
_____
_____
_____

Are athletics or physical activities a source of shame for you?

_____
_____
_____
_____
_____

Are there areas of life you are neglecting that are a cause of shame or anxiety to you?

_____
_____
_____
_____
_____

What would it be like to connect to those around you without bringing up the areas in which you are an expert?

_____
_____
_____
_____
_____

Do you feel like there is "not much of you to go around"?

_____
_____
_____
_____
_____

When do you most feel like you need to protect your resources?

_____
_____
_____
_____
_____

What kind of knowledge are you "greedy" for?

_____
_____
_____
_____
_____

Are you greedy with your time? Who will you give your time to?

_____

_____

_____

_____

_____

Do you get stuck in preparation mode? When do you usually feel prepared enough to take action?

_____

_____

_____

_____

_____

What kinds of things give you self-esteem?

_____

_____

_____

_____

_____

When have you most felt like a loner or misfit? When have you most felt like you belonged?

_____

_____

_____

_____

_____

What types of situations cause you to detach emotionally?

_____

_____

_____

_____

_____

Do you find yourself becoming absent minded? When have you forgotten to take care of your emotional or physical needs?

_____

_____

_____

_____

_____

Do you find yourself compartmentalizing your relationships or emotions?

_____

_____

_____

_____

_____

Does theorizing, speculating or fantasizing get in the way of addressing more serious issues that are going on in your life?

_____

_____

_____

_____

_____

Are you attracted to the "dark side" of life? What from your childhood or past do you attribute to this attraction?

_____

_____

_____

_____

_____

When you are stressed do you tend to retreat into the sanctuary of your mind or do you involve yourself in endless activities?

_____

_____

_____

_____

_____

Who could you reach out to when you are feeling vulnerable or afraid? How would this be different for you from going inward?

_____
_____
_____
_____
_____

What would going to therapy be like for you? What initial feelings come up? How could this benefit you?

_____
_____
_____
_____
_____

How have you handled grief in the past? Do you have any grief that is still unresolved?

_____
_____
_____
_____
_____

Have you maintained your childlike curiosity?

_____
_____
_____
_____
_____

How has being able to see many sides of things served you?

_____
_____
_____
_____
_____

What are your main coping skills when things get tough? Are they healthy or unhealthy?

_____

_____

_____

_____

_____

When do you feel most connected to your present moment?

_____

_____

_____

_____

How do you recharge after taxing social engagements?

_____

_____

_____

_____

_____

Type 6//The Loyalist

When do you become fearful, alarmed or anxious?

_____

_____

_____

_____

_____

When do you question and doubt your internal dialogue?

_____

_____

_____

_____

_____

How do you magnify situations in your mind?

_____

_____

_____

_____

_____

How do you project your positive or negative feelings onto others?

_____

_____

_____

_____

_____

When has fear of making a wrong decision held you back?

_____

_____

_____

_____

_____

When do you feel most distrustful of authority?

_____

_____

_____

_____

_____

Do you hide your emotions from everyone around you except those you are closest to?

_____

_____

_____

_____

_____

Do you feel more secure doing what is expected of you instead of striking out on your own?

_____

_____

_____

_____

_____

How has following the rules impacted you? When is it ok not to follow the rules?

_____

_____

_____

_____

_____

Who do you look up to the most in life?

_____

_____

_____

_____

_____

Do you find yourself forming strong impressions of people that are hard to shake after you have made up your mind about them?

_____

_____

_____

_____

_____

How do you feel about making big decisions? Is it difficult for you to be decisive?

_____
_____
_____
_____
_____

Do others view you as nervous, anxious or jittery? How does that impact your relationships?

_____
_____
_____
_____
_____

When do you find yourself being suspicious of others or questioning their motives? How does this affect your relationships?

_____
_____
_____
_____
_____

Would others describe you as a hard worker? Is it important to you to be viewed this way?

_____
_____
_____
_____
_____

When does your anxiety get in your way?

_____
_____
_____
_____
_____

Do you find yourself hanging onto relationships longer than others would?

_____
_____
_____
_____
_____

Do you fear being abandoned?

_____
_____
_____
_____
_____

In what ways are you lacking self-confidence?

_____
_____
_____
_____
_____

Do you have confidence in your own intuition and inner voice? How do you connect to and trust this voice?

_____
_____
_____
_____
_____

What is security to you? When will you know you have enough security?

_____
_____
_____
_____
_____

Is "belief" hard for you to achieve?

_____
_____
_____
_____
_____

How do you relate to the statement, "If I don't trust myself, then I have to find something in this world I can trust"?

_____
_____
_____
_____
_____

Who are the "authorities" in your life? This could be anyone whose opinion your trust or anyone who you feel like you need approval from.

_____
_____
_____
_____
_____

What kind of anxieties did you have as a child? Do you still hold any of these today?

_____
_____
_____
_____
_____

How could you let go of the belief that you must rely on someone or something outside of yourself for support?

_____
_____
_____
_____
_____

Are you able to spot potential problems before they arise? How has this served you?

_____
_____
_____
_____
_____

Do you fear you will lose your independence while at the same time feel that you need more support from others?

_____
_____
_____
_____
_____

When do you feel the most cynical? What can you do to combat this?

_____
_____
_____
_____
_____

What or who do you look to when you feel most stressed or anxious?

_____
_____
_____
_____
_____

What worries do you have about the future?

_____
_____
_____
_____
_____

What relationships do you have that make you feel the most secure? Do you have any that you feel insecure or cynical about?

_____
_____
_____
_____
_____

When have you let an opportunity that may have resulted in growth pass you by because you were afraid or felt you needed "security"?

_____
_____
_____
_____
_____

Recall a time you took a chance on something or someone. What was the outcome?

_____
_____
_____
_____
_____

Are there areas in your life now where you know that you are resisting your true desires out of fear or doubt about yourself? How could you change this?

_____
_____
_____
_____
_____

What beliefs are you invested in? Are they political, spiritual or philosophical?

_____
_____
_____
_____
_____

Are you seen as "the responsible one" to those around you? What has this cost you?

_____
_____
_____
_____
_____

Have the "social support" system you have set up in your life really made you more secure?

_____

_____

_____

_____

_____

What would you do without one of them?

_____

_____

_____

_____

_____

In what areas of life do you most fear rejection or abandonment?

_____

_____

_____

_____

_____

What coping skills do you use to manage your anxiety? Are you actively trying to use them?

_____

_____

_____

_____

_____

Do you cope with fear by reacting to it or against it?

_____

_____

_____

_____

_____

What are your main anxiety triggers?

_____

_____

_____

_____

_____

What is the foundation of your belief system? Are these beliefs based on your own experiences or on the authority of trusted friends, books, mentors or teachings?

_____
_____
_____
_____
_____

How do you feel about structure? Does it help you when there are guidelines, rules and procedures?

_____
_____
_____
_____
_____

How do you handle change? What would help increase your flexibility in this realm?

_____
_____
_____
_____
_____

When have you felt taken advantage of?

_____
_____
_____
_____
_____

Do you often find yourself overcommitted? What boundaries could you put in place to counter this?

_____
_____
_____
_____
_____

What voices make-up your inner critic? How have these competing voices led you to become indecisive?

_____
_____
_____
_____
_____

Do you feel that you live in a constant state of danger or mishap? What danger signs are you most tuned into?

_____
_____
_____
_____
_____

When do you feel the most safe and secure?

_____
_____
_____
_____
_____

Type 7//The Enthusiast

In what ways do you forget others' feelings or needs?

_____
_____
_____
_____
_____

How do you respond to challenges or obstructions to your plans, ideas or actions?

_____
_____
_____
_____
_____

In what ways do you avoid distress, pain or negative feedback?

_____
_____
_____
_____
_____

How are you insatiable?

_____
_____
_____
_____
_____

How are you distracted by new and exciting ideas and activities?

_____
_____
_____
_____
_____

How do positive options and opportunities absorb your attention and energy?

_____

_____

_____

_____

_____

Do you consider yourself a "renaissance man/woman"?

_____

_____

_____

_____

_____

What skills have you been able to learn quickly? Would you have valued these skills more if you had struggled to acquire them?

_____

_____

_____

_____

_____

When have you struggled with what to do to define your life path? Where are you on this journey now?

_____

_____

_____

_____

_____

How have you used staying busy as a way to avoid the painful things in life?

_____

_____

_____

_____

_____

Do you feel like you can find what you are looking for in life or do you feel the need to try everything to make sure you know what is best?

_____

_____

_____

_____

_____

Do you ever try to experience many things in life as a cover for the feeling of not really getting what you want out of life?

_____

_____

_____

_____

_____

How can you connect more with your present moment? What would help ground you in the present?

_____

_____

_____

_____

_____

Do others wish you were more serious? Do you have a balance between your optimism and your ability to take things seriously?

_____

_____

_____

_____

_____

Did you feel disconnected from a nurturing figure in your childhood? How did this affect you?

_____

_____

_____

_____

_____

Were you somehow cut off from maternal nurturance at a young age? Did another sibling or crisis in the family take away from you getting the nurturance you needed?

_____

_____

_____

_____

_____

Did you decide at a young age that you had to take care of yourself? What impact has this had on you?

_____

_____

_____

_____

_____

How do you occupy your mind with distractions? What would it look like to silence some of that inner noise?

_____

_____

_____

_____

_____

Do you feel an inner conflict between wanting to move on to greener pastures and losing the connections around you?

_____

_____

_____

_____

_____

What is your relationship like with drugs and alcohol? Is it healthy or unhealthy?

_____

_____

_____

_____

_____

How have you used romantic relationships to provide excitement and newness to your life? Have you hurt others along the way?

_____
_____
_____
_____
_____

Are you materialistic? What kind of things do you splurge on that others don't?

_____
_____
_____
_____
_____

Do you have any workaholic tendencies? How have you tried to combat them?

_____
_____
_____
_____
_____

Would others describe you as blunt? How has this gotten you into trouble?

_____
_____
_____
_____
_____

Do you have too many projects on your plate right now? What would it look like to focus all of your energy on the most important one?

_____
_____
_____
_____
_____

What responsibilities do you find most burdensome?

_____

_____

_____

_____

_____

Do you ever feel bogged down by the slow pace of others? Would slowing down yourself benefit you in any way?

_____

_____

_____

_____

_____

Do you ever feel caught between your commitments and your desire to do your own thing?

_____

_____

_____

_____

_____

Do you ever feel like you are leaving a trail of loose ends around you? How could you tie some of those up?

_____

_____

_____

_____

_____

When do you get caught up in fantasizing about the future?

_____

_____

_____

_____

Do you find yourself half committing to things in case a better option comes up? Has this hurt anyone around you?

_____
_____
_____
_____
_____

In what ways do you try to escape the mundane?

_____
_____
_____
_____
_____

How does the old adage "the grass is always greener" resonate with you?

_____
_____
_____
_____
_____

When do you most experience FOMO (fear of missing out)?

_____
_____
_____
_____
_____

How do you handle your boredom? Is this healthy or unhealthy?

_____
_____
_____
_____
_____

How have you sought out temporary relief from your anxiety? How did this work for you?

_____
_____
_____
_____
_____

How do you act as an "energizer, catalyst or spark plug" in social situations?

_____
_____
_____
_____
_____

Has your desire to make others happy had any negative consequences on you and your own happiness?

_____
_____
_____
_____
_____

Do you feel the pressure to entertain, dazzle and charm those around you? Do you find it satisfying or does it feel like you have to put on a show?

_____
_____
_____
_____
_____

How have you tried to fill your inner emptiness with external gratifications?

_____
_____
_____
_____
_____

How have you kept your mind full in order to avoid your anxieties? How do you feel when you sit with uncomfortable thoughts?

_____
_____
_____
_____
_____

How can you pursue choices that will give you long-term gratification instead of instant gratification?

_____

_____

_____

_____

_____

_____

Are you open to the advice of others? Whose advice do you most value?

_____

_____

_____

_____

_____

_____

What is your relationship like with money? Do you ever feel that your pursuit of pleasure gets in your way of being financially wise?

_____

_____

_____

_____

_____

_____

What is one way that you could slow down today?

_____

_____

_____

_____

_____

_____

How many partially finished projects do you have going right now? Is there one what you could finish today?

_____

_____

_____

_____

_____

_____

Does your overbooked schedule ever get in the way of you actually enjoying the things you're committed to?

_____

_____

_____

_____

_____

Do you ever feel deeply impatient or frustrated with yourself? What bringing up these emotions for you?

_____

_____

_____

_____

_____

Do you ever find yourself looking at tragedies in a positive light to escape the harder feelings you might experience?

_____

_____

_____

_____

_____

Do you have underlying feelings of frustration about different areas in your life? Do others view this as self-centeredness?

_____

_____

_____

_____

_____

How does staying in constant motion help you to suppress feelings such as guilt, heartbreak and regret?

_____

_____

_____

_____

_____

When have you been impulsive? How has this affected you or those around you?

_____
_____
_____
_____
_____

What are you trying to escape from in life? How has this served you?

_____
_____
_____
_____
_____

How does the phrase "enjoy now, pay later" resonate with you?

_____
_____
_____
_____
_____

Do you need more and more of an experience for it to be as stimulating as the last time?

_____
_____
_____
_____
_____

Make a list of projects you started and completed and ones you started and abandoned. Do you see any similarities in these lists? What enables you to follow through on a project?

_____
_____
_____
_____
_____

When stressed do you feel like you are the only one who can get the job done?

_____
_____
_____
_____
_____

When stressed do you feel the need to educate others? Does your passion for the topics you bring up ever turn to critique or debate?

_____

_____

_____

_____

_____

What are you most afraid of in life? How do you cope with this fear?

_____

_____

_____

_____

_____

How could you let yourself more fully process hard feelings you come across in life? What would this be like for you?

_____

_____

_____

_____

_____

Do you have "instant expert" syndrome? How does this serve you?

_____

_____

_____

_____

_____

Are you able to find the joy in the everyday things? How could you start doing this more?

_____

_____

_____

_____

_____

Do you have a meditation practice? If not how could you incorporate this into your routine?

_____

_____

_____

_____

_____

How does your joyful spirit impact others? Do you feel the need for this joyfulness to be seen and appreciated by those around you?

_____

_____

_____

_____

_____

Do you have a sense of abundance about your life and the opportunities around you? Do the people in your life share this same outlook?

_____

_____

_____

_____

_____

How could you slow down?

_____

_____

_____

_____

_____

How could you cultivate a quieter, and more focused mind?

_____

_____

_____

_____

_____

"Fulfillment is not the result of getting anything, it is the result of opening ourselves up to our present moment". How does this quote resonate with you?

_____

_____

_____

_____

_____

Is it easier for you to stay in your present moment or get caught up planning what your future could be like?

_____

_____

_____

_____

_____

When do you feel most connected to nature, to the people around you? What do these experiences do for you?

_____

_____

_____

_____

_____

How can you experience more joy in your life? How could you give more joy to others?

_____

_____

_____

_____

_____

Type 8//The Challenger

When do you just go for what you want without thinking?

_____
_____
_____
_____
_____

In what ways do you assert control, power or a sense of justice over others?

_____
_____
_____
_____
_____

How do you divert attention away from your own fears of being hurt?

_____
_____
_____
_____
_____

In what ways do you forget to be sensitive or tender toward yourself and others?

_____
_____
_____
_____
_____

Where in life are you most afraid of being controlled? Is it romantically, socially, sexually, financially or otherwise?

_____
_____
_____
_____
_____

Where in life do you feel most powerful?

_____
_____
_____
_____
_____

How does your big energy express itself?

_____
_____
_____
_____
_____

Where in life do you wish you were more independent?

_____
_____
_____
_____
_____

What is a time when you went against the status quo?

_____
_____
_____
_____
_____

Do you overlook your health for the sake of getting things done?

_____
_____
_____
_____
_____

Could you be gentler with yourself?

_____
_____
_____
_____
_____

How have you sought vengeance on yourself? What about on others?

_____
_____
_____
_____
_____

Do you find yourself rejecting others before they can reject you?

_____
_____
_____
_____
_____

What types of situations make you shut down and put your defenses up?

_____
_____
_____
_____
_____

What is your greatest accomplishment in life thus far?

_____
_____
_____
_____
_____

Do you often find yourself being the one to make the final decision when you are in a group setting?

_____
_____
_____
_____
_____

Who do you want to protect?

_____
_____
_____
_____
_____

What would life look like if you were a little less driven?

_____
_____
_____
_____
_____

How do you ignore your physical needs?

_____
_____
_____
_____
_____

Where in life you do shy away from vulnerability?

_____
_____
_____
_____
_____

Where in life do you shut down emotionally?

_____
_____
_____
_____
_____

Did you feel the need to fight to survive as a child?

_____
_____
_____
_____
_____

As a child did you feel it was unsafe to be gentle or giving?

_____
_____
_____
_____

Did you have any big moments or rejection or betrayal as a child? How has that affected you?

_____
_____
_____
_____
_____

Did you get punished frequently as a child? How did you react to the punishments?

_____
_____
_____
_____
_____

When do you feel you can let your guard down? Is it a person, a place or a pet that helps you to feel less inhibited?

_____
_____
_____
_____
_____

Did you feel like the "black sheep" or the "problem child" in your family? Do you still revert to that role when you are with your family now?

_____
_____
_____
_____
_____

Did you ever make known the "hidden" family issues that no one else would bring up? How did that affect your family dynamics?

_____
_____
_____
_____
_____

Do you feel like you "lost your innocence" as a child?

_____
_____
_____
_____
_____

Do you feel the need to protect yourself from others in fear of losing your independence?

_____
_____
_____
_____
_____

Who can you trust to support you? Do you feel that you lose your autonomy when you ask them for help?

_____
_____
_____
_____
_____

Do you find yourself fed up with people who are overly "nice"? What are their intentions?

_____
_____
_____
_____
_____

Where are you most independent in life? Where do you look to others for help?

_____
_____
_____
_____
_____

Do you have a hard time taking orders from others? Who is the hardest to take orders from in life right now?

_____
_____
_____
_____
_____

How does your driven mindset impact your work and vocational life? What would happen if you didn't push yourself so hard?

_____
_____
_____
_____
_____

How does physical activity affect your mood? Is this something you need to incorporate into your daily life?

_____
_____
_____
_____
_____

Where does life feel out of control right now? How have you taken steps to remedy this?

_____
_____
_____
_____
_____

What would it be like for you if you let go of control of your environment? Have you ever had a time you had to do this? What was that like for you?

_____
_____
_____
_____
_____

Do you relate to the statement "I am assertive, direct and resourceful"?

_____
_____
_____
_____
_____

Are you a competitive person? Where does this most manifest itself in your life?

_____
_____
_____
_____
_____

Do you worry that those around you do not respect you? Can you think of anyone specific who you feel this way about?

_____
_____
_____
_____
_____

In what ways do you protect yourself from others? What would it look like to let your guard down?

_____
_____
_____
_____
_____

How are you protective of your resources? Does this get in the way of being generous?

_____
_____
_____
_____
_____

How could you be gentler with those around you?

_____
_____
_____
_____
_____

When have you pushed others to their limit? How can you avoid this in the future?

_____
_____
_____
_____
_____

What do you fear will happen if you do not protect yourself?

_____
_____
_____
_____
_____

How does the statement, "I lose interest if I win too easily" resonate with you?

_____
_____
_____
_____
_____

What qualities do you most respect in others? What about in yourself?

_____
_____
_____
_____
_____

When do you most feel the need to control others?

_____
_____
_____
_____
_____

Do you find yourself using more energy than needed for any given activity? What would it be like if you didn't use such force? Would your activity still be completed?

_____

_____

_____

_____

_____

Who can you share your fears and doubts with? How do you feel after you do this?

_____

_____

_____

_____

_____

Identify one person, place or time in your life you have not felt the need to be tough. How is this different than other areas of your life?

_____

_____

_____

_____

_____

When do you feel most alive?

_____

_____

_____

_____

_____

How has your desire for intensity impacted how you live and the choices you make?

_____

_____

_____

_____

_____

Do you consider yourself a "daredevil"? Has this gotten you into any trouble in the past?

_____

_____

_____

_____

_____

Do you push past health concerns that others would probably address? How has this impacted your overall health?

_____

_____

_____

_____

_____

How does the sense of aliveness you get from taking risks and pushing limits different from the sense of aliveness you get from relaxing? What does this do to your sense of self?

_____

_____

_____

_____

_____

When has your lust for a person, for money for power or for sex completely controlled you?

_____

_____

_____

_____

_____

How do you cope when you feel like you don't have control in life? Are these coping skills positive or negative?

_____

_____

_____

_____

_____

Do you have an entrepreneurial spirit? What would having the independence, respect and power you want be like for you?

_____

_____

_____

_____

_____

Do you feel the need to run every part of your life all alone? Where could you ask for help?

_____

_____

_____

_____

_____

How would asking for help feel to you?

_____

_____

_____

_____

_____

How do others react to the way you intensely discuss or argue your point? Do they shut down or are they up for the challenge?

_____

_____

_____

_____

_____

When you find yourself in an argument where do you hold your tension in your body?

_____

_____

_____

_____

_____

Do you hide how much stress you are under from others? What would it be like to share this with someone else?

_____
_____
_____
_____
_____

Are you taking any steps to take care of your health or are you waiting until something becomes an issue to address it?

_____
_____
_____
_____
_____

When you put yourself under tremendous pressure, who are you doing it for? What would have happened if you were easier on yourself?

_____
_____
_____
_____
_____

When has your forthright way of speaking gotten you into trouble with other enneagram types? Is there a type you have a hard time connecting to?

_____
_____
_____
_____
_____

How do you test the boundaries of others?

_____
_____
_____
_____
_____

Do you intimidate others? How did you become aware of this?

_____

_____

_____

_____

_____

When eights feel threatened or insure they can come unpredictable, impulsive and explosive. Can you think of a time when this played out in your own life? What would have prevented it?

_____

_____

_____

_____

_____

Who have you had a hard time taking direction from? What about this person was a trigger for you?

_____

_____

_____

_____

_____

Have you dismissed other's emotional pain because you have ignored your own emotional reactions over the years? How could this change?

_____

_____

_____

_____

_____

When have you defied the authorities around you? This could be a parent, teacher, church leader or boss.

_____

_____

_____

_____

_____

Can you remember an incident from childhood where you would not back down? How did you feel emotionally?

_____
_____
_____
_____
_____

When eights bite off more than they can chew they retreat to five where they go in stress to strategize, buy time and then come back for more. Do you find this to be true? Can you describe a time where you have done this?

_____
_____
_____
_____
_____

When have you become deeply preoccupied with your plans and projects and worked relentlessly until they were done? Do you ever keep these plans a secret from those around you?

_____
_____
_____
_____
_____

When you are stressed do you find yourself turning inward, sizing up your situations and making a plan before you can re-engage?

_____
_____
_____
_____
_____

Write down a few times you have felt rejected. Do you still hold onto any of these situations in present day? How did these situations affect you?

_____
_____
_____
_____
_____

Have you suffered from thoughts of those you love turning against you? Are these thoughts rational?

_____

_____

_____

_____

_____

Have you allowed yourself to fully grieve any losses you have experienced? How was the grieving process for you?

_____

_____

_____

_____

_____

Do you assume that others do not want to hear your feelings or troubles? What would it look like to open up to one person today?

_____

_____

_____

_____

_____

How is your work-life balance? How could you take steps to improve it?

_____

_____

_____

_____

_____

What injustices do you feel fired up about? What could you do to help fight against them?

_____

_____

_____

_____

_____

What person, community or group do you feel most passionate about influencing for the better?

_____
_____
_____
_____
_____

How do you divert attention away from your own fears of being hurt?

_____
_____
_____
_____
_____

Type 9//The Peacemaker

In what ways do you just go along with others' agendas?

_____

_____

_____

_____

_____

How do you get distracted from your real priorities?

_____

_____

_____

_____

_____

How are you stubborn?

_____

_____

_____

_____

_____

How do you respond when you feel tension, discomfort or conflict?

_____

_____

_____

_____

_____

What makes you angry?

_____

_____

_____

_____

_____

How do you make those around you feel safe?

_____
_____
_____
_____
_____

How does being "comfortable" pay a role in your life?

_____
_____
_____
_____
_____

Would you rather let someone else have their way than create a scene? Why is this?

_____
_____
_____
_____
_____

Are you an optimist or a pessimist?

_____
_____
_____
_____
_____

How have you struggled to form your own identity?

_____
_____
_____
_____
_____

Do spiritual concepts and spirituality come easily to you?

_____
_____
_____
_____
_____

Do you only feel "good" when those around you feel "good"?

_____

_____

_____

_____

_____

What role do daydreams of fantasies play in your life? Do these move you towards or away from action?

_____

_____

_____

_____

_____

When have you numbed your pain? How did this turn out for you?

_____

_____

_____

_____

_____

In childhood did you take on the peacemaker or mediator role in your family? How did this affect you?

_____

_____

_____

_____

_____

In childhood did you fade in to the background or become the "low maintenance child"? How did this affect you?

_____

_____

_____

_____

_____

Do you feel in touch with what you really want in any given situation? What would help you connect to this inner knowing?

_____

_____

_____

_____

_____

When have you felt guilty for having needs of your own?

_____

_____

_____

_____

_____

What painful memories or experiences have you repressed?

_____

_____

_____

_____

_____

Do you find yourself avoiding your anxieties by doing busy work?

_____

_____

_____

_____

_____

When do you get caught up in passive-aggressive behaviors? How could you resolve this?

_____

_____

_____

_____

_____

How have you handled conflict in the past? Do you usually get the outcome you are looking for?

_____

_____

_____

_____

_____

How do you handle change? Do you worry change will disrupt your inner-peace?

_____

_____

_____

_____

_____

Do you often find yourself going along with things you really do not want to do? How does the effect your involvement in the activity?

_____

_____

_____

_____

_____

What things in life excite you the most? Is this type of energy or excitement hard for you to tap into on a daily basis?

_____

_____

_____

_____

_____

When have you been lazy or slothful about dealing with internal issues? What about external issues?

_____

_____

_____

_____

_____

How have you focused more on others than on yourself in the past?

_____

_____

_____

_____

_____

Have you ever mistaken numbness for relaxation? How do you differentiate between the two?

_____

_____

_____

_____

_____

Do you find yourself checking out? Have you ever checked out for a long span of time? How did you come out of this?

_____

_____

_____

_____

_____

How do you relate to the statement, "I do not have to be in constant contact with somebody as long as they are there"?

_____

_____

_____

_____

_____

Do you idealize any of your relationships, with your partner, family, coworkers? How does this allow you to focus on others instead of on yourself?

_____

_____

_____

_____

_____

When you idealize others what traits do your often focus on? Do you feel that you lack these traits?

_____

_____

_____

_____

_____

How could you strengthen your intuition or inner voice?

_____
_____
_____
_____
_____

What role has spirituality, wisdom or religion played in your life? What aspects have hurt you?

_____
_____
_____
_____
_____

What aspects have helped you?

_____
_____
_____
_____
_____

Are you willing to seek peace at any cost? When could seeking peace be a bad thing?

_____
_____
_____
_____
_____

Who threatens your peace the most? How do you cope with this?

_____
_____
_____
_____
_____

How do you react when you get too excited about something? Does this also feel like a danger to your inner peace?

_____
_____
_____
_____
_____

Do you find yourself living vicariously through others?

_____
_____
_____
_____
_____

Where in life are you "hitting the snooze button"? Have you been putting off any goals that you have?

_____
_____
_____
_____
_____

What underlying feelings of resentment or rage have you been pushing down?

_____
_____
_____
_____
_____

Do you find yourself focusing on work when worries and anxieties surface?

_____
_____
_____
_____
_____

Do you find yourself often deflecting compliments or downplaying your achievements?

_____
_____
_____
_____
_____

Do you feel comfortable saying "no" to others? Who do you need to have better boundaries with?

_____

_____

_____

_____

_____

Do you find yourself checking out when you spend time with others? How could you be more present with the people around you?

_____

_____

_____

_____

_____

How has your ability to be patient served you?

_____

_____

_____

_____

_____

How could you invest more in your personal development?

_____

_____

_____

_____

_____

Do you feel that your participation in the world is unimportant? What do you do to combat these thoughts?

_____

_____

_____

_____

_____

How do you connect to the world around you? Is it nature, good conversations, the ability to be quite, the beauty your find in everyday life or something else entirely?

_____
_____
_____
_____
_____

How do you love the people around you?

_____
_____
_____
_____
_____

When do you feel most loved by the people around you?

_____
_____
_____
_____
_____

Made in the USA
Columbia, SC
23 December 2020

29829856R00065